555 Sticker Fun Pirate Ship

Licensed exclusively to Top That Publishing Ltd
Tide Mill Way, Woodbridge, Suffolk, IP12 1AP, UK
www.topthatpublishing.com

4 6 8 9 7 5
Manufactured in China

In the rigging

The pirate ship is sailing away on a new adventure. Fill the rigging with stickers of pirates, climbing up to unroll the ship's sails.

The crow's-nest

The pirate in the crow's-nest is on lookout duty. Add stickers of things he needs to help him do his job.

The captain's cabin

The captain is busy working in his cabin. Use the stickers to fill the room with lots of his belongings. Can you spot his two pets?

Sleeping quarters

It is night-time in the pirates' sleeping quarters. Add stickers of sleepy pirates to the hammocks and find places for their things. They don't have as *much* as the captain!

The cannon deck

Today, the pirates are busy on the cannon deck. Fill the deck with cannons, cannonballs and pirates getting ready for action.

The map room

This is where the pirates plan their treasure-hunting trips.
Find spaces for all their navigating gear.

N
V
Ö
S

At the helm

Steering the ship is an important job. It is a lonely job, too! Add some creatures to keep the pirate company.

The armoury

This is where the pirates store their weapons. Add stickers of busy pirates stocking the shelves with all the things they use for fighting. Add extra weapons, too.

The training deck

The pirates train here every week to improve their fighting skills. Fill the training deck with stickers of pirates working out and plenty of extra equipment.

Treasure trove

The pirates' treasure is kept in here under lock and key. Fill the room with booty from dreadful pirate deeds.

In the workshop

There are lots of mending jobs to do on a pirate ship. Fill the workshop with stickers of all the tools and equipment that pirates need for fixing things.

Pirates' pantry

The pirates' pantry needs filling with supplies. Add stickers to fill the shelves with food to last for the whole trip.

The ship's galley

It is hard work feeding a ship full of hungry pirates. Fill the galley with more food, plates and kitchen utensils.

The games deck

This is where the pirates have fun in their free time. Fill the games deck with competing pirates and lots of games to choose from.

The laundry

It is wash day in the laundry. Use stickers to fill the room with drying clothes and things the pirates need for washing, drying and ironing. Take extra care with the captain's uniform!

The pirates' mess

In the evening, the pirates have supper in the ship's mess. Make sure that everyone has cutlery. Add extra food, too.

The sick-room

Even pirates get ill sometimes! Add one more ailing pirate to the sick-room scene. Stock the shelves with pills, potions and first-aid kit.

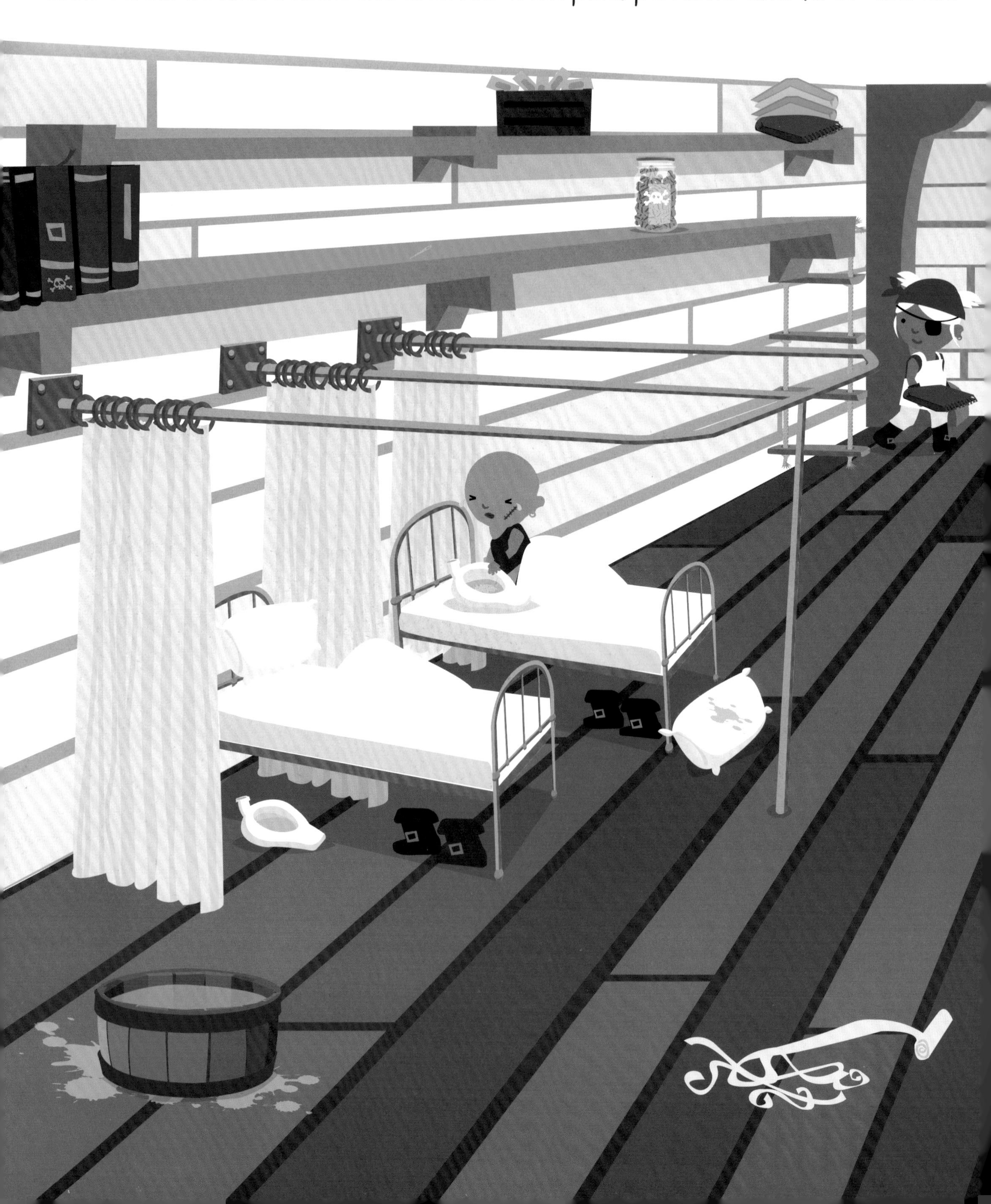

Scrubbing the decks

Once a week, the pirates have to scrub the decks! Complete the scene with pirates lugging water buckets and scrubbing on their hands and knees.

The captain's aviary

The captain loves exotic birds. Fill his aviary with the beauties that he has collected on his travels. Can you find the sticker of the hungry cat? This spells trouble!

In the bilge

The bilge is at the bottom of the ship. Fill the damp room with pirates emptying out water from rain, leaks and spillages. They hate this smelly job!

The fishing deck

The pirates like to fish when the weather is fine. Fill the fishing deck with pirate fishermen and greedy seabirds. Can you spot the ship's cook at work?

Pirate portraits

The pirates are very proud of their fearsome ancestors. Use stickers to fill the ship's gallery with portraits of famous pirates of the past.

In the cells

Traitors and baddies beware! A week in the cells is enough for any pirate
Add chains and keys to the scene, as well as some mice!

The pirates' snug

On dark, cold nights, the pirates relax in the cosy snug. Add stickers of pirates enjoying their hobbies and things that make the place feel like home.